From Mama's Kitchen

Whether we're young or old or somewhere in between, there's a very close tie between generations that makes the years vanish . . . and so very often it centers about the kitchen, the dining room table . . . those times when the family is all together.

And then one recalls a special person, a special phrase, a special recipe . . . my own Mother saying, "I can do it myself" . . . my Grandmother saying, "It won't take a minute to make the dumplings" . . . my great Grandmother saying, "the bread sauce will be ready in a moment" . . .

And with each generation the memories are the same: we, too, want to create the recipes that express our own individuality . . . something we've made to share with our family and friends . . . not something purchased, but the results of our own efforts . . . just as our mothers, grandmothers, and great-grandmothers did . . . perhaps something whose beginning is found in our back-yard garden.

Assembled in this cookbook are some of those very special handed-down-from-generation-to-generation recipes which were created by hand . . . with each generation adding a little personal touch of its own . . .

. . . to which *we've* added a little bit of poetry and prose, a touch of photography and art . . . to make this FROM MAMA'S KITCHEN a very special Ideals cookbook for you.

Catherine Smith
author

Maryjane Hooper Tonn
editor

Second Printing

CONTENTS

IDEALS PUBLISHING CORP., MILWAUKEE, WIS. 53201
© COPYRIGHT MCMLXXVI, PRINTED AND BOUND IN U.S.A.
ISBN 0-89542-641-2 195

Potato Salad

Salads

RHUBARB SALAD

2 c. fresh rhubarb slices, 1 inch thick
⅓ c. sugar
½ c. water
2½ c. pineapple tidbits in syrup
1 pkg. raspberry gelatin
1 pkg. lemon gelatin
½ c. chopped nuts

Combine rhubarb and sugar; cook in water until tender. Drain, reserving syrup. Drain pineapple and reserve syrup. Combine syrups and add water to make 3½ cups. Heat to boiling. Add both packages of gelatin and stir until dissolved. Chill until syrupy. Fold in rhubarb, pineapple and nuts. Pour into a 6-cup ring mold. Chill until firm. Unmold. Serve with mayonnaise as a salad or with whipped cream as a dessert.

MANDARIN BEAN RELISH

1 1-lb. can cut green beans
½ c. mandarin orange segments
3 T. sliced celery
¼ c. diced onion
½ t. sugar (more, if desired)
½ t. salt
　Dash of pepper
2 T. vinegar
¼ c. salad oil

Drain beans. Combine in shallow dish with orange segments, celery and onion. Combine all remaining ingredients in a jar; cover and shake to blend. Pour over bean mixture. Cover and chill several hours, stirring occasionally.

TUNA-FRUIT SALAD

1 7-oz. can tuna, drained
1 unpeeled apple, chopped
1 c. seedless grapes, halved
1 13½-oz. can pineapple tidbits, drained
1 c. chopped celery
1 T. lemon juice
¼ t. salt
1 c. sour cream
　Salad greens
　Chopped nuts

In a bowl, combine tuna, apple, grapes, pineapple and celery. In a small bowl, gently blend lemon juice and salt into sour cream. Fold into fruit. Serve on greens and top with chopped nuts.

POTATO SALAD

8 medium potatoes	½ t. salt
¼ c. chopped onion	¼ t. seasoned salt
6 slices bacon	1 c. mayonnaise
4 eggs, hard-boiled	¼ c. sweet pickle relish

Boil potatoes until done. Cool and dice. Add onion. Fry bacon until crisp. Crumble into potatoes. Add eggs, seasonings, mayonnaise and relish. Mix well and chill.

BEET SALAD

2 c. beets, cooked and diced
1 c. beet juice, chilled
1 pkg. lemon gelatin
1 c. boiling water
½ c. diced celery (optional)
1 small can crushed pineapple, drained

Dissolve gelatin in boiling water. Add chilled beet juice and stir in. Add diced beets, celery and pineapple. Chill until set. Serve with a bit of sour cream on top.

TASTY FRENCH DRESSING

1 can condensed tomato soup
1 c. salad oil
¾ c. vinegar
½ c. sugar
1 t. dry mustard
1 t. paprika
1 t. salt
1 t. celery seed
2 cloves garlic, crushed

Mix all ingredients in a fruit jar and shake.

HOLIDAY SALAD

1 c. coarsely chopped cranberries
5 c. shredded cabbage
1 T. grated orange peel
2 T. sugar
½ t. salt
⅓ c. mayonnaise

Mix first 5 ingredients, tossing well. Add mayonnaise and mix. Cover and chill before serving.

MACARONI SALAD

1 1-lb. package macaroni
1 tomato, chopped
1 c. celery, finely chopped
3 hard-boiled eggs, chopped
1 c. mayonnaise
1 c. shredded cheese
   Salt and pepper to taste

Cook macaroni according to directions on package. Drain and cool. Add tomato, celery, eggs, mayonnaise, cheese and seasonings. Mix well. Chill and serve.

BEAN-BEET SALAD

2 1-lb. cans green beans
2 1-lb. cans shoestring beets
2 small onions

Drain green beans and beets. Slice onions into thin rings. Toss lightly.

DRESSING

½ c. salad oil
⅔ c. vinegar
   Salt and pepper to taste
1 t. Worcestershire sauce
½ c. sugar
1 small clove garlic *or* dash of garlic salt

Mix ingredients for dressing. Let vegetables marinate in dressing 4 or 5 hours before serving.

PICKLED BEET SALAD

2 pkg. lemon gelatin
2 c. hot water
1 T. lemon juice
2 pt. pickled beets
1½ c. diced celery
½ c. chopped nuts
1 t. horseradish
   Pinch of salt

Dissolve gelatin in hot water. Add lemon juice. Drain pickled beets, reserving 2 cups liquid. Add liquid to gelatin. Dice beets. Chill gelatin until partially set and then add remaining ingredients. Chill.

Soups

HAMBURGER SOUP

1½ lbs. hamburger
1 small onion, diced
3 carrots, sliced
2 c. chopped celery stalks and leaves
2 potatoes, peeled and cubed
½ c. barley
½ t. garlic salt
½ t. salt
¼ t. pepper

Crumble hamburger into a saucepan. Add all other ingredients. Cover with water and bring to boil. Cook slowly until vegetables and barley are well done—about 1½ hours.

NAVY BEAN SOUP

1 lb. navy beans
2 qt. cold water
   Ham hocks or meaty ham bones
1 chopped onion
½ c. chopped celery tops (optional)
1 bay leaf

Wash beans, add cold water and soak overnight. Add remaining ingredients the next morning; bring to a boil. Turn heat to simmer, cover and cook about 3 hours. Remove ham hocks, chop the meat, and return to the soup. Season to taste. Note: More water may have to be added during the cooking process.

CHEESE SOUP

2 T. chopped onion
4 T. butter or margarine
4 T. flour
¼ t. salt
¼ t. dry mustard
2 c. milk
2 c. chicken broth or bouillon
2 c. grated cheddar cheese

Brown onion in butter. Blend in flour and seasonings. Gradually stir in milk and broth. Bring to a boil and boil 1 minute, stirring constantly. Add cheese. Cook slowly, stirring constantly, until cheese is melted.

TURKEY SOUP

2 c. cooked, chopped turkey meat
1 T. chopped onion
½ c. chopped celery
2 carrots, washed and diced
2 potatoes, peeled and diced
½ t. seasoning salt
½ t. salt

Combine all ingredients in a saucepan, cover with water, and cook together until vegetables are well done. Some water may have to be added while cooking. Serve hot with your favorite crackers. An excellent way to use leftover Thanksgiving turkey.

6

Pictured opposite
Cheese Soup

Fruits and Vegetables

FRIED EGGPLANT

1 eggplant
1 egg
1 T. cold water
¾ c. fine bread crumbs
½ t. salt
  Dash of pepper
½ c. fat or oil

Wash and pare eggplant. Cut in half, then into long slices, ½ inch thick by 1 inch wide. Beat egg. Add water. Dip eggplant into egg, then into combined bread crumbs and seasonings. Cook slices in hot oil, browning on both sides. Drain on paper. Serve at once.

TURNIP CASSEROLE

3 c. sliced turnips
2 t. sugar
½ t. salt
2 to 2½ c. water
  Milk
3 T. butter or margarine
3 T. flour
½ c. crushed dry cereal
2 T. melted butter
2 tablespoons grated cheese

Cook turnips with sugar and salt in just enough water to cover. Drain, reserving liquid. Measure and add enough milk to make 1½ cups. Melt 3 tablespoons butter; blend in flour. Pour in liquids and cook, stirring, until thickened. Combine with turnips in greased baking dish. Cover with cereal, 2 tablespoons butter, and cheese. Bake at 325° about 25 minutes, or until brown.

FRIED GREEN TOMATOES

6 green tomatoes
3 T. flour
1¼ t. salt
1¼ t. sugar
  Pepper to taste
4 T. bacon fat
1 c. evaporated milk

Wash but do not peel tomatoes. Cut in halves crosswise. Mix flour, salt, sugar and pepper. Roll tomatoes, one at a time, in flour. Brown on both sides in hot bacon fat. Remove to hot serving dish and keep warm. Add evaporated milk to the same frying pan. Boil slowly, stirring constantly until thick (about 2 minutes). Pour over tomatoes.

SCALLOPED POTATOES

6 to 8 medium potatoes
1 T. minced onion
  Salt and pepper to taste
2 c. milk
½ c. grated cheese

Wash, pare and thinly slice potatoes. Arrange in layers in greased baking dish. Sprinkle each layer with a bit of onion, salt and pepper. Heat milk and pour over potatoes but do not fill to top of potatoes. Bake uncovered at 350° for about 1 hour and 15 minutes. Crumble grated cheese on top and bake 10 minutes longer.

SCALLOPED CORN

2 c. fresh or canned corn
1 c. milk
1 c. cracker crumbs
2 T. diced onion
2 eggs, well beaten
1 t. salt
  Pepper to taste
2 T. melted butter

Combine all ingredients and pour into a buttered baking dish. Bake at 350° for 1 hour.

CANDIED SWEET POTATOES

6 medium sweet potatoes or yams
¾ c. brown sugar
¼ c. butter
1 t. salt
5 or 6 marshmallows, if desired

Wash and boil sweet potatoes in enough water to cover until just tender. As soon as they are cool enough, peel and cut in ½-inch slices. Place in buttered baking dish. Sprinkle brown sugar and salt over slices and dot with butter. Bake at 375° about 30 minutes. Top with marshmallows the last 5 minutes. Variation: 1 cup drained crushed pineapple may be spread over the slices of sweet potato, then the brown sugar and butter.

QUICK BAKED BEANS

2 large (#2½) cans pork and beans
2 T. chopped onion
½ c. brown sugar
¼ c. dark corn syrup or mild sorghum
½ c. tomato catsup
4 slices bacon

Combine all ingredients except bacon slices. Pour into baking dish. Arrange bacon slices over the top. Bake uncovered for 2 hours at 325°.

CORN PUDDING CASSEROLE

3 eggs
2 c. drained cooked or canned corn
2 c. milk, scalded
1 T. melted butter
1 t. salt
2 T. chopped onion

Beat eggs. Add corn. Gradually stir in scalded milk. Add remaining ingredients and mix well. Pour into 1½-quart buttered casserole. Set in shallow pan and fill pan to 1 inch with hot water. Bake in preheated oven at 350° for 45 minutes, or until knife inserted near center comes out clean. Let stand 5 minutes and serve hot.

NINE DAY PICKLES

7 lbs. cucumbers (small to medium)
1 pt. (2 cups) coarse salt
1 gallon boiled and cooled water
2 c. vinegar
8 green grape leaves
1 t. alum

Wash cucumbers and place in stone jars in brine made of the salt and water. Let stand 4 days, then drain. Cover with clear, fresh water each morning for 3 consecutive days. Wash and split each pickle, regardless of size. Put in kettle with the vinegar and enough water to cover the pickles. Add grape leaves and alum and simmer for 2 hours. Do not boil. Drain and place in stone jars.

SYRUP

3 pt. vinegar (6 cups)
6 c. sugar
1 oz. whole allspice

Boil vinegar, sugar and allspice to make a syrup. Pour over pickles and let stand overnight. Pour off liquid, reheat and pour over again. Let stand overnight and on the third morning put pickles in hot sterilized jars. Heat the same liquid, pour over pickles, and seal immediately.

BREAD-AND-BUTTER PICKLES

3 qt. sliced cucumbers
3 onions, sliced
½ c. coarse salt
3 c. vinegar
1 c. water
3 c. sugar
1 t. cinnamon
½ t. ginger
2 T. mustard seed
2 t. turmeric
½ T. celery seed
1 piece horseradish (optional)

Mix cucumbers, onions, and salt. Let stand at least 5 hours. Drain. Boil vinegar, water, sugar and seasonings for 3 minutes. Add cucumbers and onions and simmer 10 to 20 minutes. Do not boil. Pack into hot sterilized jars and seal immediately.

LIME SWEET PICKLES

7 lbs. cucumbers
2 c. hydrated lime
2 gallons water
2 qt. vinegar
9 c. sugar
1 T. salt
1 t. celery seed
1 t. whole cloves
1 t. mixed pickling spice

Slice cucumbers thin. Cover with the lime and water and soak 24 hours. Drain. Rinse and soak 3 hours in clear water. Drain and rinse again. Bring remaining ingredients to a boil. Pour over cucumbers and soak overnight. Bring to a boil. Boil gently 40 minutes. Pack in hot sterilized jars and seal. Note: Be sure to soak all the lime out.

GRAPE CONSERVE

8 c. Concord grapes
3 c. water
4 c. sugar
1 c. raisins
½ c. orange juice
¼ c. lemon juice
½ c. nuts
¼ t. salt

Wash grapes. Add water and simmer, covered, for 30 minutes. Press skins and pulp through a coarse strainer. Only the seeds should be discarded. Add remaining ingredients and boil 15 minutes or until thick.

CRISPY LUNCH PICKLES

25 medium-sized cucumbers
8 large onions
2 large sweet peppers
½ c. salt
5 c. sugar
5 c. cider vinegar
2 T. mustard seed
1 t. turmeric
¼ t. cloves

Wash fresh cucumbers and slice thin. Chop onions and peppers. Mix with cucumbers and salt; let stand for 3 hours. Drain. Combine sugar, vinegar and spices in large kettle. Bring to a boil. Add drained cucumbers; heat thoroughly but do not boil. Pack while hot into hot sterilized jars and seal at once.

TOMATO CATSUP

1 bushel tomatoes	2 t. celery seed
1 doz. onions	2 t. allspice
3 green peppers	5 c. sugar
2 t. mixed pickling spices	1 qt. vinegar
2 t. cinnamon	2 t. red pepper
4 sticks cinnamon	4 T. salt
2 t. cloves	⅔ c. cornstarch
2 t. dry mustard	

Wash and cook tomatoes, onions and green peppers until tender. Run through sieve, discarding seeds and skins. Place sieved pulp in large cooking kettle. Tie all spices in a cloth bag and drop into pulp. Add sugar, vinegar, red pepper and salt. Cook all together and boil ½ hour. Add cornstarch dissolved in small amount of cold water. Stir in, cook until thickened, and seal while hot.

PUMPKIN BUTTER

10 c. raw pumpkin
2 lemons
1 t. ground ginger
1 t. ground cinnamon
½ t. ground allspice
¾ t. salt
2½ lbs. brown sugar
1 c. water

Peel pumpkin and grind in food chopper. Extract juice from lemons; add to pumpkin along with spices, salt and sugar. Let stand overnight. Then add water and boil gently until pumpkin is clear and the mixture is thick. Pour into sterilized jars and seal while hot. This is good on toast.

PICCALILLI

1 gallon green tomatoes, chopped
2 T. coarse salt
1 gallon cabbage, finely chopped
1 qt. onions, finely chopped
2 or 3 green peppers, finely chopped
½ T. cinnamon
1 T. ground mustard
1 t. ginger
1 T. cloves
1½ oz. turmeric
½ oz. celery seed
6 c. sugar
　Vinegar

Chop green tomatoes, sprinkle with salt, and let stand 2 hours. Drain. Mix tomatoes with other vegetables. Add spices and sugar and mix well. Cover with vinegar (not too much) and boil slowly until vegetables are done. Seal while hot.

STRAWBERRY LEMON PRESERVES

4 c. fresh strawberries
4 c. sugar
2 T. lemon juice

Heat berries and 2 cups of the sugar to the boiling point, stirring occasionally. Boil 2 minutes. Add remaining sugar and again heat to boiling. Boil 3 minutes. Stir in lemon juice and pour into shallow bowl. Stir occasionally while cooling. Let stand overnight to plump berries.

GREEN PEPPER RELISH

1 large head cabbage
½ doz. medium onions
1 doz. sweet green peppers
1 T. mustard seed, mashed
1 T. celery seed
½ t. black pepper
4 c. water
1 qt. white vinegar

Finely chop the cabbage, onions and peppers. Mix and let stand several hours in a little salt water. Drain. Add remaining ingredients and mix well. Do not cook.

Yeast Breads

EASY ROLLS

2 c. milk
¼ c. sugar
¼ c. shortening
1 pkg. yeast
   Flour
1 t. baking powder
½ t. baking soda
1 t. salt

Scald milk. While cooling, add sugar and shortening. When cool, add yeast and enough flour to make a batter. Let rise about 1½ hours. Add baking powder, soda, and salt and enough flour to make a soft dough. Roll out on lightly floured board, cut like biscuits, place on greased baking sheet and let rise until doubled. Bake at 375° about 25 minutes.

BASIC ROLLS

1 c. sugar
¼ c. shortening
1 t. salt
2 c. boiling water
2 pkg. yeast
¼ c. warm water
1 T. sugar
2 eggs, beaten
8 c. flour

Mix sugar, shortening, salt and boiling water together. Cool. Dissolve yeast in ¼ cup warm water and stir in 1 tablespoon sugar. Add to cooled first mixture. Beat in eggs and 4 cups flour. Add remaining 4 cups flour and mix to make a smooth dough. Knead slightly. Shape into rolls, allow to double in bulk and bake at 425° for about 20 minutes. This dough may be kept in refrigerator, covered, for a week to 10 days. A good basic dough for rolls, coffee cake or cinnamon rolls.

QUICK ROLLS

2 c. milk
4 T. sugar
1 pkg. yeast
4 T. melted fat
1 t. salt
6 c. flour (approximately)

Scald milk and cool to lukewarm. Dissolve yeast and sugar in the lukewarm milk. Add melted fat and salt and 3 cups flour. Beat until very smooth. Cover and let rise in a warm place for one hour. Add enough flour to make a firm dough. Let rise again for 30 to 45 minutes. Make into rolls or shape into balls about the size of walnuts. Cover and let rise to the top. Bake at 350° for 20 minutes. Remove from oven and brush tops with butter.

*Pictured opposite
Yeast Breads and Rolls*

ONION BREAD

1 c. warm water
1 pkg. yeast
2 t. sugar
½ t. salt
1 onion, grated
2½ c. flour
1 onion, grated

Dissolve yeast in warm water. Add sugar and salt and blend in. Beat in 2 cups of the flour and mix well. Add remainder of flour and grated onion. Turn dough onto lightly floured board and knead until smooth—5 to 7 minutes. You may have to add up to ½ cup more flour while kneading. Place dough in greased bowl and set in a warm place to rise until doubled in size. Punch down and divide in half. Place in 2 greased 9-inch cake pans and brush tops with melted buter. Let rise 5 minutes. Punch dough down again and let rise until double. Dust with paprika. Bake at 375° for 20-25 minutes.

WHITE BREAD

2 c. warm water or potato water
3 T. butter
½ c. sugar
1 T. salt
2 pkg. yeast
6½ to 7 c. flour

Dissolve yeast in ¼ cup of the water. Heat remainder of water with sugar, butter and salt. Cool to lukewarm. Add dissolved yeast and stir. Add 4 cups flour and beat well. Add the remaining flour 1 cup at a time. Knead on lightly floured board. Let rise in greased bowl until doubled in size. Punch down, shape into loaves, and let rise again. Bake at 375° for 5 minutes, then at 350° for 30 minutes.

ANADAMA BREAD

½ c. yellow cornmeal
2 c. water
1 t. salt
2 T. shortening
1/3 c. molasses
1 pkg. yeast
5 cups flour (approximately)

Stir cornmeal into water and salt. Mix well and bring to a boil, stirring constantly. Lower heat and cook 5 minutes. Add shortening and molasses; cool. When lukewarm, add yeast that has been dissolved in ½ cup warm water. Add enough flour to make a stiff dough. Place in greased bowl and let rise until double. Bake at 400° for 1 hour. Butter when removed from oven and cover with a cloth.

BATTER BREAD

1 c. milk
2 T. shortening
3 T. sugar
1 t. salt
1 c. lukewarm water
2 pkg. yeast
4½ c. flour

Scald milk. Add shortening, sugar and salt; cool to lukewarm. Measure warm water into a large bowl. Dissolve yeast in water. Add lukewarm milk mixture. Stir in enough flour to make a stiff batter. Beat about 2 minutes. Cover and let rise in a warm place about 40 minutes, until more than doubled in bulk. Stir batter down and beat vigorously ½ minute. Pour into 2 greased 9" x 5" x 3" loaf pans. Bake at 375° about 50 minutes.

FRENCH BREAD

1¼ c. warm water
1 pkg. yeast
1 T. shortening
1 T. sugar
1½ t. salt
3½ c. flour

Measure water into a large bowl. Add the yeast and stir until dissolved. Add shortening, sugar and salt. Stir in flour. Turn out onto a lightly floured board. Knead until the dough is springy and elastic. Place in a greased bowl and brush the top lightly with shortening. Cover and let rise in a warm place until doubled in bulk. Punch down. Let rise again until doubled. Punch down and turn out onto a floured board. Cut into 2 equal portions. Roll each half into an oblong, 8" x 10". Beginning with the wide side, roll up tightly and seal the edge by pinching. Lengthen and taper loaves. Place loaves on a greased baking sheet and sprinkle lightly with cornmeal. Brush with a cornstarch glaze made by mixing 1 teaspoon cornstarch with 2 tablespoons water. Let rise 1½ hours. Take a sharp knife and make ¼-inch-deep slashes at 2-inch intervals. Bake at 375° for 45 minutes.

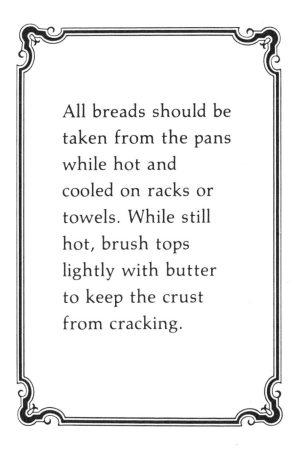

All breads should be taken from the pans while hot and cooled on racks or towels. While still hot, brush tops lightly with butter to keep the crust from cracking.

DANISH PASTRY

1 c. sugar
½ t. salt
3 eggs, beaten
½ c. butter
2 t. vanilla
2 pkg. yeast
8 c. flour
½ lb. butter

Heat the first 5 ingredients together for one minute, and then add yeast which has been dissolved in 2 cups lukewarm water. Add flour. Mix in thoroughly and knead until smooth. Let rise for 1 hour in a warm place. Roll out 1 inch thick. Dot with butter, fold together four times, roll out to same thickness. Continue this procedure until one-half pound of butter has been added to the dough. Form into any shape of rolls desired. Let rise one hour before baking. Bake 25 to 35 minutes in 400° oven.

Quick Breads

SKILLET CAKE

¼ c. butter
¾ c. brown sugar
8 canned pineapple slices
1 c. nutmeats
2 eggs
1 c. granulated sugar
¼ t. salt
½ c. milk
1 T. melted shortening
1 c. sifted cake flour
1 t. baking powder
1 t. vanilla

Melt butter in iron skillet. Remove from heat. Sprinkle brown sugar over the bottom and arrange pineapple slices. Sprinkle with nuts. Beat eggs until light. Gradually add granulated sugar and salt. Heat milk to the boiling point. Add shortening and beat into the egg mixture. Add flour and baking powder sifted together. Beat in vanilla. Pour batter over fruit. Bake about ½ hour at 350°. Turn out while hot and serve upside down.

BANANA NUT BREAD

1 c. sugar
½ c. shortening
2 eggs
1 c. mashed bananas
1 t. lemon juice
2 c. flour
1 T. baking powder
½ t. salt
1 c. chopped nuts

Cream the sugar and shortening. Add eggs and beat well. Add bananas and lemon juice. Sift dry ingredients together and add to banana mixture. Add nuts. Bake in greased loaf pan at 350° for one hour.

APPLE NUT BREAD

1 c. sugar
½ c. shortening
2 eggs
1 c. grated raw apples (unpeeled)
2 c. flour
1 t. baking powder
1 t. baking soda
¼ t. salt
½ c. nuts

Cream sugar and shortening. Add eggs and beat well. Mix in grated apple. Sift dry ingredients together and add to first mixture. Add nuts and mix well. Bake in greased loaf pan at 350° for 50 to 60 minutes.

18

Pictured opposite
Banana Nut Bread

BROWN BREAD

1½ c. buttermilk
1½ t. baking soda
½ t. salt
1½ c. thick molasses or sorghum
4 c. whole wheat flour
1 c. raisins (optional)

Mix buttermilk, soda and salt. Add molasses, then flour, and mix well. Add raisins if desired. Pour into well-greased coffee cans, filling ⅔ full. Set in boiling water. Let water come within 1½ inches of top of can. Boil about 2 hours. Test done with toothpick.

COFFEE CAKE

¾ c. sugar
½ c. shortening
1 t. vanilla
3 eggs
2 c. flour
1 t. baking soda
1 t. baking powder
1 c. sour cream

Combine sugar, shortening and vanilla; mix well. Add eggs, one at a time, beating well after each. Sift dry ingredients together. Add to egg mixture alternately with sour cream. Spread half of batter in greased tube pan. Spread half of topping on batter, cover with remaining batter, and top with remaining topping.

TOPPING

1 c. brown sugar
6 T. butter
2 t. cinnamon
1 c. chopped nuts

Cream together brown sugar and butter. Add cinnamon and chopped nuts and mix well. Bake at 350° for 50 minutes.

RICH COFFEE CAKE

1 c. shortening
1 c. brown sugar
1 c. white sugar
2 c. flour
2 eggs
1 c. sour cream
1 t. baking soda
½ t. salt

Cream shortening and sugars together. Add flour and mix until crumbly. Set aside 1 cup of this mixture. Beat eggs. Add sour cream, soda and salt; mix well. Combine with first mixture and beat well. Pour into a greased 9" x 13" cake pan and sprinkle top with the reserved mixture. Bake at 350° for 40 minutes.

CAKE DOUGHNUTS

2 eggs
1 c. sugar
2 T. soft shortening
¾ c. buttermilk
3½ c. flour
1 t. baking soda
2 t. baking powder
¼ t. cinnamon
¼ t. nutmeg
½ t. salt

Beat eggs. Add sugar and shortening and beat. Stir in buttermilk. Sift dry ingredients and add gradually to egg mixture to make a stiff dough. Chill 2 hours. Roll out on floured board to ⅓-inch thickness. Cut with doughnut cutter. Brown on each side about one minute in 3 inches of 370° shortening in a deep saucepan. Drain on paper or towel and dust with powdered sugar.

RAISED DOUGHNUTS

1 c. mashed potatoes
1½ c. milk, scalded
½ c. sugar
⅓ c. shortening
2 eggs
¼ c. warm water
2 pkg. yeast
1 t. salt
4½ to 5 c. flour

Boil and mash potatoes and measure 1 cup into a bowl. Add milk, sugar, shortening and well-beaten eggs. When lukewarm, add flour and salt. Mix and then knead on a lightly floured board. Place in greased bowl and let rise until doubled. Roll out and cut with doughnut cutter and fry in deep hot fat.

GLAZE

1 lb. powdered sugar
1 T. cornstarch
2 T. soft butter
1 T. cream
1 t. vanilla

Combine ingredients. Stir in enough warm water to make a thick liquid. Dip warm doughnuts in glaze and let drip off.

APPLE PLUMPLINGS

2 c. flour
1 t. baking powder
1 c. milk
1 egg, beaten
6 large apples

Mix all ingredients except apples. Peel and core apples; cut into ½" cubes. Add to batter. Drop mixture into deep, hot fat by tablespoonfuls. Be sure you have some apple pieces in each spoonful. When brown, lift out of fat and place on brown paper to drain. Serve while hot.

DROP DOUGHNUTS

2 c. flour
½ c. sugar
2 t. baking powder
¼ t. baking soda
1 t. cinnamon
½ t. salt
1 egg
½ c. applesauce
½ c. milk
1½ T. melted shortening

Sift dry ingredients together. Beat egg. Add applesauce and milk. Add dry ingredients and mix well. Stir in shortening. Drop batter into hot fat (375°) by teaspoonfuls, frying until golden brown on all sides.

DOUGHNUTS

3 eggs
1 c. milk
1 c. sour cream
1 c. sugar
½ t. salt
2 t. baking powder
1 t. baking soda
½ t. nutmeg
1 c. flour

Beat eggs until light. Add milk and sour cream and blend. Sift the dry ingredients together and add to egg mixture. Beat until smooth. Add enough flour to make a soft dough. Pat out dough to ½ inch thick. Cut with doughnut cutter and fry in hot deep fat. May be rolled in sugar while warm.

BISCUITS

2 c. flour
2 t. baking powder
¾ t. salt
⅓ c. fat
¾ c. milk (approximately)

Sift dry ingredients together. Cut in fat until well blended. Stir in milk slowly, using just enough to make dough soft but not sticky. Turn dough onto lightly floured board and knead a few strokes. Roll to ½-inch thickness and cut with biscuit cutter. Place on baking sheet and bake at 450° about 15 minutes.

BAKING POWDER BISCUITS

3 c. flour
4 t. baking powder
1 t. salt
6 T. shortening
1 c. milk

Sift dry ingredients into a bowl. Cut in shortening and add milk. Stir only until moistened. Turn onto lightly floured board. Knead lightly and roll out ½ inch thick. Cut with floured biscuit cutter. Bake at 400° until lightly browned.

QUICK MUFFINS

1½ c. flour
½ t. salt
4 t. baking powder
1 T. sugar
2 eggs, well beaten
¾ c. milk
¼ c. melted butter

Sift dry ingredients together. Add eggs, milk and butter. Mix just until blended. Drop into greased muffin tins, filling ½ to ⅔ full. Bake at 425° for 25 minutes.

APPLE MUFFINS

2 c. flour
4 t. baking powder
½ c. sugar
1 t. salt
½ t. cinnamon
1 egg
1 c. milk
1 c. chopped raw apples (unpeeled)
2 T. melted shortening

Sift dry ingredients together into a bowl. In a separate bowl beat egg; add milk, chopped apples and melted shortening. Add to dry ingredients and mix lightly until blended. Fill greased muffin tins ⅔ full and bake at 425° for 20 to 25 minutes. Serve hot.

BREAKFAST MUFFINS

1½ c. flour
½ t. salt
2¼ t. baking powder
2 T. sugar
1 egg
¾ c. milk
2 T. melted butter

Sift dry ingredients together into a bowl. Beat egg in separate bowl and add the milk and butter. Add this mixture to the dry ingredients. Stir until just mixed; batter should be lumpy. Fill greased muffin tins ⅔ full. Bake at 425° for 25 minutes. Loosen from pan and serve hot with butter and jam, jelly or honey. Makes 8.

Breakfast Muffins

CRISPY CORN BREAD

1 c. flour
4 t. baking powder
1 t. salt
¼ c. brown sugar
1 c. yellow cornmeal
1 egg, well beaten
1 c. milk
¼ c. melted shortening

Sift the first three ingredients into a bowl. Add the brown sugar and cornmeal and mix. Combine egg, milk and shortening, add to dry ingredients and stir just until moist. Pour into a greased 8-inch pan and bake at 450° for 25 minutes.

DELUXE CORN BREAD

2 c. cornmeal
1 t. salt
4 T. sugar
4 T. flour
2 t. baking powder
2 c. boiling water
4 T. melted shortening
4 eggs, separated

Mix dry ingredients together. Gradually add boiling water, stirring well. Stir in shortening. Beat yolks into cornmeal mixture. Beat egg whites and fold in last. Bake in a loaf pan at 350° for 30 to 40 minutes.

Corn Bread

SWEET MILK PANCAKES

1½ c. flour
2 t. baking powder
1 T. sugar
½ t. salt
1 egg
1½ c. milk
2 T. melted buter

Sift dry ingredients together. Separate egg and beat yolk. Combine yolk with milk and melted butter; beat. Add to dry ingredients and mix well. Beat egg white until soft peaks form. Fold into batter. Bake on hot griddle. Serve with your favorite syrup.

CORN PANCAKES

1½ c. flour
1 t. baking soda
2 T. sugar
1 t. salt
½ c. yellow cornmeal
2 eggs, slightly beaten
2 c. buttermilk
2 T. melted butter or bacon fat

Sift first four ingredients into mixing bowl. Stir in the cornmeal. Add eggs, buttermilk and melted fat, stirring until flour is barely moistened. Pour batter from ¼ cup or ⅓ cup measure onto a hot, lightly greased griddle. Turn once. Serve hot.

BUTTERMILK PANCAKES

1 c. buttermilk
1 t. baking soda
¼ t. salt
¼ c. sour cream
1 egg
¼ c. quick oatmeal, uncooked
½ c. plus 1 T. flour
½ t. baking powder
⅓ c. sugar
2 T. cornmeal

Pour buttermilk into a bowl. Add soda and salt. Add sour cream and stir until it foams. Beat in egg with a spoon. Add oatmeal. Sift dry ingredients into the mixture and stir until no flour lumps remain. Fry on hot griddle. Serve with your favorite syrup, honey, jam or jelly.

FRENCH TOAST

2 eggs
1 c. milk
8 slices bread
Margarine

Beat eggs and add milk. Pour into a flat, shallow dish. Dip bread in mixture on both sides and fry in melted margarine in skillet until golden brown. Add margarine as needed. Serve toast hot with your favorite syrup.

JOHNNYCAKE

1 c. cornmeal
½ c. sugar
¼ t. salt
Lukewarm water
6 eggs
4 c. milk

Mix cornmeal, sugar and salt in large bowl. Add just enough lukewarm water to moisten the cornmeal mixture, being careful not to use enough to make mixture wet. Beat the eggs until light and foamy. Add milk. Stir milk mixture into cornmeal mixture and stir together thoroughly. Pour into two ungreased pie pans and bake at 350° until set, 30 to 40 minutes. The cornmeal settles to the bottom of the pan and the eggs and milk form a custard on top. Cut pie in wedges and serve warm with your favorite syrup.

Main Dishes

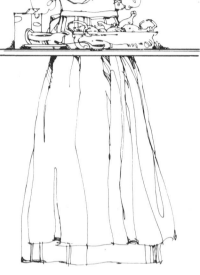

GROUND BEEF CASSEROLE

1½ lbs. ground beef
1 c. raw rice
1 onion, chopped
¼ t. diced dried garlic
1 t. salt
½ t. pepper
2½ c. tomato juice
1 c. boiling water

Brown beef, rice and onion together in frying pan, adding fat if necessary. Add seasonings, tomato juice and water. Pour into a 2-quart covered casserole. Bake for 1 hour in 300° oven.

HAMBURGER DINNER

1 lb. ground beef
1 small onion, chopped
½ c. washed raw rice
½ t. salt
Dash of pepper
2 T. chopped parsley
Flour
1 c. sliced carrots
½ c. chopped celery
1 c. green beans
2 c. tomato juice *or* tomatoes

Mix together the first 6 ingredients and shape into balls. Roll meatballs in flour and place in casserole. Arrange the vegetables between the meatballs. Pour tomato juice or tomatoes over all. Cover and bake at 325° for 1 hour. Uncover and bake 30 minutes longer.

SPINACH SPECIAL

1½ lbs. ground beef
2 onions, chopped
1 green pepper, chopped
2 c. chopped spinach
3 eggs, beaten
½ c. grated cheese
½ t. salt
Dash of pepper
½ t. oregano
¼ t. nutmeg

Brown ground beef. Sauté onions and green pepper; add to beef. Add chopped spinach. Cook over low heat just until done. Add eggs, grated cheese and seasonings. Cook until eggs are done. Serve immediately with French bread.

Spinach Special

MEAT LOAF

2 lbs. ground beef
2 T. finely chopped onion
2 eggs, well beaten
4 slices bread
¾ c. milk
1 t. salt
¼ t. pepper

Mix beef, onion and eggs. Soften bread in the milk and add to meat. Add salt and pepper and mix well. Bake in loaf pan at 325° for 1 hour.

HAM LOAF

1 lb. cured ham, ground
1 lb. fresh pork, ground
2 eggs
⅔ c. cracker crumbs or quick-cooking rolled oats
⅓ c. quick-cooking tapioca
1¼ c. milk
1 t. salt

Mix all ingredients together and form into a loaf in a loaf pan.

DRESSING

¼ c. vinegar
½ c. water
½ c. brown sugar
1 T. prepared mustard

Mix all ingredients together and boil for 5 minutes. Pour over the loaf and bake at 350° for 2 hours, basting occasionally. The dressing should become thick and syrupy.

DELUXE MEAT LOAF

2 lbs. ground beef
2 eggs, beaten
2 c. bread crumbs
5 T. chopped onion
1 t. salt
¼ t. pepper
¼ t. dry mustard
¼ t. sage
¼ t. chili powder
½ c. tomato puree
½ finely chopped celery

Mix together all ingredients. Blend thoroughly. Pack into greased loaf pan, shaping into a loaf. Bake at 350° about 1½ hours, or until well done.

SALMON LOAF

1 1-lb. can salmon
2 T. soft butter or margarine
1 T. lemon juice
1 T. finely chopped onion
1 t. parsley flakes
¼ t. oregano
Dash of pepper
2 T. flour
2 eggs

Mix salmon, butter or margarine, lemon juice and onion. Combine seasonings and flour and add to salmon. Beat eggs until light and fluffy and fold in. Pour into greased baking dish and bake at 350° for 45 minutes.

SKILLET DINNER

½ lb. ground beef
1 c. finely diced onion
2 T. fat
¼ t. garlic salt
½ c. uncooked rice
5 to 6 cups water
1 c. finely diced carrots
1 c. finely diced potatoes
1 t. soy sauce
1 t. salt
  Pepper to taste

Brown ground beef and onion in fat. Sprinkle with garlic salt. Add rice and water and simmer uncovered over low heat for 40 minutes. Add carrots and potatoes and continue to simmer until tender, adding more water if necessary. Add seasonings. Serve hot.

MARINATED MEATBALLS

1½ lbs. ground chuck
1 large egg, beaten
¼ c. fine, dry bread crumbs
1 t. salt
  Dash of pepper
½ c. salad oil
2 T. chopped parsley
1 T. chopped onion
½ t. celery salt
¼ t. salt
¼ t. garlic powder

Combine meat, egg, bread crumbs, salt and pepper. Shape into 1½-inch balls. Place in bowl. Mix remaining ingredients and pour over meatballs. Refrigerate for 3 to 5 hours. Broil in oven. Turn and baste with marinade as often as meat appears dry.

Variety may be added to fish by sprinkling with tarragon, marjoram or curry powder before cooking.

BARBEQUE HAMBURGER (FOR FIFTY)

8 lbs. ground beef
2 t. salt
½ c. shortening or oil
1½ c. chopped onion
1½ c. chopped celery
½ c. brown sugar
2 T. prepared mustard
½ c. vinegar
2 qt. tomato sauce

Brown the beef in a heavy skillet, stirring to keep crumbly. Add the salt. In another skillet, melt shortening and sauté onion and celery until tender. Add to hamburger. Add remaining ingredients and simmer for 15 minutes. Serve on hot hamburger buns.

OVEN-COOKED CHICKEN IN SOUR CREAM

1 cut-up frying chicken, 2½ to 3 pounds
1 c. sour cream
1 t. Worcestershire sauce
1 t. lemon juice
1 t. celery salt
1 t. paprika
½ t. salt
¼ t. pepper
1 c. fine bread crumbs
⅓ c. melted butter or margarine

Combine sour cream with seasonings. Dip chicken pieces in sour cream mixture. Coat pieces in bread crumbs. Pour melted butter into baking pan. Place chicken pieces in pan skin side up. Bake in 400° oven for 1 hour or until tender.

BEEF SCRAMBLE

1 T. fat
½ lb. ground beef
¼ c. chopped onion
½ t. salt
  Pepper to taste
3 eggs
2 T. cold water

Mix beef, onion, salt and pepper; brown in the fat. Drain. Beat eggs slightly with the water. Pour over the cooked beef and cook over low heat just until eggs are set. Serve on hot buttered toast.

GRANDMA'S GOULASH

½ lb. ground beef
½ c. chopped onion
1 t. salt
¼ t. pepper
4 c. cooked tomatoes
1 c. uncooked macaroni

Brown ground beef and onion. Add seasonings and tomatoes and bring to a boil. Add macaroni. Simmer until macaroni is done, stirring often.

SMOTHERED CHICKEN

1 2½ to 3-pound frying chicken, prepared for frying
1½ c. flour
1 t. salt
¼ t. pepper
1 t. minced onion
2 to 3 c. hot milk
¾ c. hot fat

Mix flour, salt and pepper. Roll chicken pieces in mixture until coated; brown quickly in skillet in hot fat. Place in baking dish, sprinkle with minced onion and cover with hot milk. (There should be enough to cover chicken.) Bake at 350° for 1½ hours. If chicken becomes dry during first hour, dot with butter and add a little more hot milk. By the time it is ready to serve, the chicken should have completely absorbed the milk.

Pictured opposite
Oven-Cooked Chicken in Sour Cream

STUFFED CABBAGE LEAVES

8 large cabbage leaves
1 lb. ground beef
1 beaten egg
½ t. salt
¼ t. pepper
1½ c. finely chopped celery
1 T. chopped onion
1 c. bread crumbs
1 large tomato, peeled and chopped, *or*
    ¾ c. canned tomatoes
2 T. brown sugar
3 T. lemon juice
1 c. beef broth or bouillon
¼ t. salt

Cook cabbage leaves in a large kettle of slightly salted water just until cabbage is limp (about 3 minutes). Drain. Combine ground beef, egg, salt, pepper, celery, onion and bread crumbs. Place about ⅓ cup of the meat mixture in center of each cabbage leaf. Fold the sides over the filling, then fold over the ends. Place in a large skillet with the seam side down. Mix the remaining ingredients and pour over the rolls. Cover and simmer 45 minutes, occasionally spooning the sauce over the rolls.

SPANISH RICE

1 lb. ground beef
2 T. onion, finely chopped
¼ c. green pepper, finely chopped
2 t. brown sugar
1 t. salt
¼ t. pepper
½ t. chili powder
4 c. canned tomatoes
½ c. catsup
¾ c. uncooked rice

Cook ground beef, onion, green pepper, brown sugar, salt, pepper and chili powder in heavy frying pan until beef is browned. Add tomatoes and catsup, then the uncooked rice. Cover and simmer until rice is tender—about 40 minutes—stirring occasionally.

STUFFED BAKED SQUASH

2 acorn squash
2 c. chopped ham
1 c. crushed pineapple
2 T. brown sugar

Wash squash and split them in half lengthwise. Clean out and wash seed cavity. Place cut side down on a baking sheet and bake at 350° for 30 to 40 minutes. Remove from oven. Turn cut side up. Mix ham, pineapple and brown sugar. Place equal portions of the mixture in the squash halves. Return to oven and bake 25 to 30 minutes longer, or until squash is tender.

TUNA CASSEROLE

2 7-oz. cans tuna, flaked
2 eggs, beaten
2 T. chopped onion
2 T. chopped celery
1 c. cooked peas
1 t. salt
¼ t. pepper
1 T. Worcestershire sauce
1 c. quick-cooking rolled oats
1 c. milk

Combine all ingredients. Pour into a well-greased casserole dish. Bake at 350° for 50 minutes or until set.

BAKED HOMINY

1½ lbs. ground beef
1 T. diced onion
1 T. flour
1 t. salt
¼ t. pepper
2 c. canned tomatoes
2 T. fat
1 large can hominy (2½ c.), drained
¼ lb. American cheese, grated

Brown beef and onion. Add flour, seasonings, and tomatoes. In a separate skillet, brown the hominy in the fat. Add to meat mixture. Place in a greased casserole and sprinkle with grated cheese. Bake at 350° for 30 minutes.

CHILI CON CARNE

2½ c. uncooked pinto beans
  or 2 1-lb. cans red kidney beans
1½ lbs. ground beef
  1 c. chopped onion
  ½ c. chopped green pepper
  4 c. canned tomatoes
  1 6-oz. can tomato paste
2½ t. chili powder
  1 bay leaf
  ¼ t. cumin
  1 t. salt

Soak the pinto beans overnight in 6 cups water. Or bring beans and water to a boil, cover, and let stand 1 hour. In either case, simmer for 2 hours or until tender. Drain, reserving 1 cup of the liquid. Cook and stir ground beef, onion and green pepper in a large skillet until meat is brown and onion and peppers are tender. Add all the rest of ingredients and the 1 cup of bean liquid; cover and simmer for 1 hour. Serve with hot cornbread made from your favorite recipe.

BAKED LIVER WITH VEGETABLES

1½ lbs. sliced beef liver
  ¾ c. flour
  ½ t. salt
    Dash of pepper
  2 T. fat
  2 small onions, thinly sliced
  4 small carrots, pared and chunked
  2 c. tomatoes
  2 c. mashed potatoes

Dredge liver with seasoned flour. Brown in hot fat, adding a little more fat if necessary. Place browned slices in a greased casserole. Add onions and carrots; pour tomatoes over all. Cover and bake at 350° for one hour. While the liver is baking, boil 3 or 4 medium-sized pared potatoes. Drain and mash, adding ¼ cup milk and 1 teaspoon butter; beat until fluffy. Cover the baked liver with the hot mashed potatoes. Bake at 400° until the potatoes are brown.

BROWNED HASH

2 c. cooked meat, chopped (beef, turkey, ham, chicken or lamb)
2 c. boiled potatoes, chopped
1 T. chopped onion
  Salt and pepper to taste
1 T. minced parsley (optional)
1 c. milk
2 T. fat

Mix all ingredients except milk and fat. Melt fat in a heavy skillet over medium heat. When the fat is very hot, spread hash mixture evenly in the skillet. The bottom of the hash should brown quickly. Add the milk and mix. Cover and cook slowly until crisp, about 10 minutes.

CHICKEN PIE

  1 frying chicken, cut up *or* chicken parts
  ½ t. salt
  ¼ t. pepper
  1 t. chopped parsley

Wash chicken thoroughly and cut up, trimming off any excess fat. Place in pan with a tight cover. Add just enough water to cover the chicken pieces. Add seasonings. Bring to a boil, then reduce heat to keep bubbling; cover and cook until tender, about 40 minutes. Cool. Pick all meat from the bones and chop into small chunks.

GRAVY

Measure the remaining broth in which the chicken was cooked. For each cup of broth, mix smooth ¼ cup cold water and 1 tablespoon flour. Stir the flour and water into the broth; heat to a boil, stirring constantly. Add chopped chicken. Pour the chicken mixture into a Dutch oven or a large baking pan, such as a cake pan. Top with your favorite baking powder biscuit dough, cutting small rounds of dough and placing on top of the chicken. Bake in preheated 400° oven until the biscuit topping is browned, about 12 to 15 minutes. Serve piping hot.

ICE CREAM

4 eggs
1 c. sugar
  Dash salt
1 qt. light cream or half-and-half
1 c. whipping cream
1 c. milk
2 T. vanilla

Beat eggs. Add sugar and salt and mix well. Add all liquids and vanilla. Freeze in hand-turned or electric ice-cream freezer according to manufacturer's directions.

ICE CREAM TOPPING

2 c. applesauce
1/3 c. red cinnamon candies
2 T. sugar
1 T. lemon juice

Combine all ingredients. Heat to melt candies. Cool and chill. Stir before spooning over vanilla ice cream.

MARSHMALLOW SNOW

1/2 c. milk
30 large marshmallows
1 c. whipping cream
1 c. crushed pineapple, drained

Melt marshmallows in milk. Cool. Whip cream until stiff. Add marshmallow mixture and whip together until stiff. Fold in pineapple. Chill overnight. Cut in squares to serve.

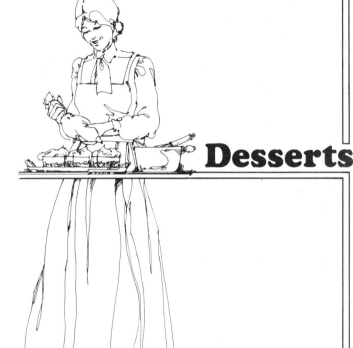

Desserts

PEANUT BUTTER FUDGE

2 c. brown sugar
1/8 t. salt
2 T. light corn syrup
3/4 c. milk
4 T. peanut butter
1 t. vanilla

Combine brown sugar, salt, corn syrup and milk. Cook to soft ball stage (test in cold water). Cool to lukewarm. Add peanut butter and vanilla. Beat until the gloss is gone. Pour into 8" square pan. When set, cut into squares.

APPLE PANDOWDY

1 c. brown sugar
¼ c. flour
¼ t. salt
1 t. vinegar
1 c. water
1 c. flour
2 t. baking powder
¾ t. salt
¼ c. butter or margarine
¾ c. milk
5 c. pared, sliced apples
¼ t. cinnamon
Dash of nutmeg
1 t. lemon juice
1 t. vanilla
2 T. butter, melted

Mix sugar, flour and salt in a saucepan. Stir in vinegar and water. Cook over low heat, stirring constantly, until thickened. Set aside. Heat oven to 375°. Sift flour, baking powder and salt together. Cut in shortening. Add milk and stir until moistened. Arrange apple slices in well-greased 8" x 12" x 2" baking dish. Add cinnamon, nutmeg, lemon juice, vanilla and butter to sauce. Pour over apples. Drop dough on top of apples. Bake 40 minutes or until topping is brown. Serve warm. Serves 6

STRAWBERRY-RHUBARB COBBLER

2 c. sugar
¼ c. quick-cooking tapioca
¼ t. salt
3 c. fresh rhubarb, cut into 1-inch pieces
3 c. halved strawberries
2 T. butter
1½ c. flour
1 T. sugar
¼ t. salt
3 t. baking powder
¼ t. cream of tartar
⅓ c. shortening
½ c. milk

Combine sugar, tapioca, salt, rhubarb and strawberries in an 8-inch square baking dish. Let stand about 15 minutes. Then dot with butter and bake at 400° for 15 minutes. While fruit mixture bakes, sift together dry ingredients. Cut in shortening until mixture resembles coarse crumbs. Add milk and stir until all is moistened and clings together when pressed into a ball. Pat or roll on floured board into an 8-inch square. Cut into 9 squares and place squares on top of hot fruit. Bake at 400° for 30 minutes or until brown.

MARSHMALLOW-POPCORN BALLS

6 qts. popped corn
½ c. butter
1 lb. marshmallows

Melt butter in double boiler. Add the marshmallows and stir until melted. Pour over the popped corn and stir until well mixed. Form into balls.

KOOL-AID SHERBET

1 c. sugar
1 pkg. Kool-Aid
3 c. milk

Dissolve sugar and Kool-Aid in the milk. Pour into refrigerator freezing tray. Freeze until partially firm. Spoon into cold bowl and beat with an eggbeater until smooth but not melted. Return to tray. Freeze until firm, about 2 hours. Makes ¾ quart.

APPLE BROWN BETTY

2 c. finely chopped apples
½ c. brown sugar
½ c. bread crumbs
½ c. chopped nuts
½ t. cinnamon
2 T. butter

Place a layer of apples in a greased baking dish. Mix dry ingredients together. Sprinkle apples with the mixture. Alternate layers until all is used, ending with the crumbs on top. Dot with butter. Cover and bake at 350° for 45 minutes. Uncover to brown. Serve warm or cold with cream.

APPLE-NUT COBBLER

½ c. sugar
½ t. cinnamon
1 c. nutmeats
4 c. pared, thinly sliced, tart apples
1 c. flour
1 c. sugar
1 t. baking powder
¼ t. salt
1 egg, well beaten
½ c. evaporated milk
⅓ c. butter or margarine, melted

Mix sugar, cinnamon and ½ cup of the nuts. Place apple slices in bottom of 8-inch round baking dish. Sprinkle with the cinnamon mixture. Sift dry ingredients together. Combine egg, milk and melted butter. Add dry ingredients and mix until smooth. Pour over apples. Sprinkle with the remaining nuts. Bake at 325° for about 55 minutes.

QUICK COBBLER

3 to 4 c. canned fruit (any kind)
⅓ c. sugar
½ c. butter or margarine
1 c. flour
1 c. sugar
2 t. baking powder
1 t. salt
1 c. milk

Heat fruit in its syrup with ⅓ cup sugar. Stir until sugar is dissolved. Melt butter in 9" x 13" pan. Mix flour, sugar, baking powder, salt and milk. Pour into pan. Then pour fruit over the batter. Bake at 350° for 1 hour.

APPLE DUMPLINGS

1½ c. sugar
1½ c. water
¼ t. cinnamon
¼ t. nutmeg
½ t. red food coloring
2 T. butter
2 c. flour
2 t. baking powder
1 t. salt
⅔ c. shortening
½ c. milk
6 medium apples, pared and cored

Combine sugar, water, spices and food coloring; bring to a boil and add butter. Cool. Sift dry ingredients together. Cut in shortening until mixture resembles coarse meal. Add milk and stir just until flour is moistened. Roll on lightly floured board into rectangle about 18" x 12" x ¼". Cut into 6-inch squares. Place a whole apple in each square. Sprinkle generously with sugar. Dot with butter. Moisten edges of squares. Fold in corners to center and pinch edges together. Place 1 inch apart in baking dish. Pour the syrup over the dumplings. Bake at 375° for 35 minutes or until apples are tender. Serve with cream.

DUTCH CRACKER PUDDING

2 c. salted crackers
4 c. milk
3 eggs, separated
½ c. sugar
1 c. flaked coconut
1½ t. vanilla
6 T. sugar

Break crackers into coarse crumbs; set aside. Scald milk in 3-quart saucepan. Beat egg yolks until light. Add hot milk to yolks, stirring well. Return to saucepan. Stir in ½ cup sugar and cook about 2 minutes, stirring constantly. Add cracker crumbs and coconut. Cook and stir until crumbs are soft and pudding has thickened. Stir in vanilla and pour into lightly buttered baking dish, about 8 inches square. Beat egg whites until frothy. Gradually add the 6 tablespoons sugar, beating until the mixture holds stiff peaks. Spread over pudding and swirl. Bake at 350° until meringue is brown, about 15 minutes. Cool to serve.

STRAWBERRY SHORTCAKE

2 c. flour
3 t. baking powder
½ t. salt
5 T. sugar
½ c. shortening
1 egg, beaten
⅓ c. milk
4 c. sweetened, crushed strawberries
1 c. cream

Mix flour, baking powder, salt and sugar. Cut in the shortening until mixture has the texture of cornmeal. Add egg and then enough milk to make the dough easy to handle. Roll or pat dough into rounds for individual shortcakes (about ½ inch thick). Place on cookie sheet and bake at 450° for 12 to 15 minutes. Split shortcakes, cover with strawberries, and serve with cream.

DATE PUDDING

½ c. chopped, pitted dates
⅓ c. sugar
3 T. cornstarch
¼ t. salt
2¼ c. milk
1½ t. vanilla
¼ c. chopped nuts
1 c. whipped cream (optional)

Combine dates, sugar, cornstarch and salt in a saucepan. Add milk. Stir and cook until the mixture is smooth and thick. Boil vigorously for about 1 minute. Remove from heat and add vanilla and nuts. Chill and serve topped with whipped cream.

CARROT PUDDING

½ c. sugar
½ c. butter
2 eggs
1 c. grated raw carrots
1 c. grated raw potatoes
1 t. baking soda
2 T. hot water
1½ c. flour
½ t. nutmeg
½ t. cinnamon
½ t. cloves
½ t. salt
½ c. raisins, washed and drained

Cream sugar and butter. Beat in eggs. Add grated vegetables and soda dissolved in hot water. Sift dry ingredients together, combine with raisins, and add to first mixture. Mix thoroughly. Pour into buttered double boiler. Steam for 2 to 3 hours.

RICE PUDDING

¼ c. uncooked rice
2 c. milk
½ t. salt
2 eggs, separated
2 T. butter
½ c. sugar
1 T. lemon juice
1 c. raisins
½ t. mace
½ c. whipping cream

Wash rice. Soak in milk for 30 minutes in top of double boiler. Add salt. Cook over hot water until rice is tender and milk is almost all absorbed, stirring often. Beat egg yolks. Add a little hot rice to egg yolks and stir in. Add to mixture in double boiler. Cook 2 minutes, stirring. Cream butter and sugar. Blend in lemon juice and mace. Stir in washed and drained raisins. Add to rice mixture and blend well. Whip cream and fold in. Beat egg whites until they form soft peaks. Fold into rice mixture. Turn into buttered 1-quart casserole. Bake at 325° for 30 minutes or until set. Serve warm or cold with cream, if desired.

CREAMY BAKED CUSTARD

2 eggs (or 4 egg yolks)
⅓ c. sugar
¼ t. salt
2 c. milk, scalded
1 t. vanilla

Beat eggs slightly. Add sugar and salt and beat well. Add scalded milk gradually, stirring constantly. Stir in vanilla. Pour into lightly buttered 5-6-ounce custard cups. Place in warm water in a shallow pan. Bake at 350° for 25 or 30 minutes, or until a silver knife inserted 1 inch from edge of dish comes out clean.

CANNED CHERRY PIE

Pastry for 2-crust 9-inch pie
1 c. sugar
3 T. cornstarch
Dash of salt
4 c. pitted cherries
6 to 8 drops red food coloring
½ t. almond extract
1 T. butter

Roll pastry and line pie pan. Mix sugar, cornstarch, and salt together. Pour cherries into heavy saucepan. Add sugar mixture and food coloring and stir in. Cook over medium heat, stirring constantly, until thick. Add extract and butter. Pour into pastry-lined pan. Top with slitted crust, seal edges, and bake at 400° until nicely browned.

Pies

BUTTERMILK PIE

1 c. sugar
1½ T. flour
1½ c. buttermilk
1½ t. lemon extract
¼ t. salt
1½ t. lemon juice
3 eggs, beaten
1 t. grated lemon rind
1 unbaked 8-inch pie shell

Combine sugar and flour. Add buttermilk, lemon extract, salt, lemon juice and beaten eggs. Mix well. Pour into pastry-lined pan. Sprinkle top with grated lemon rind. Bake at 425° until inserted knife comes out clean.

PLAIN PIE CRUST

2 c. flour
¾ t. salt
¾ c. shortening
5 T. cold water

Sift flour and salt together into a bowl. Cut in shortening with a pastry blender. Add water and mix just until mixture will hold together. Divide dough into two parts. Roll out on floured board to desired size, being careful to use no more flour than absolutely necessary. Fit into pans, press edges and cut off excess dough. Prick dough in pan with a fork. Bake at 400° until lightly browned. Makes 2 single crusts or one double-crust pie.

MINCEMEAT

1 lb. beef
½ lb. suet
4 lbs. apples
½ lb. currants
1 lb. raisins
1½ lbs. brown sugar
1 qt. cider
1 c. meat stock
2 t. salt
1 t. cloves
1 t. nutmeg
2 t. cinnamon
5 T. lemon juice

Grind beef and suet (or use 1½ pounds fatty ground beef). Pare, core and chop apples. Chop together currants and raisins. Mix apples, currants, raisins, sugar, cider and meat stock. Cook about 5 minutes. Add beef, suet and seasonings to apple mixture. Simmer 1 hour, stirring frequently to keep from burning. Add lemon juice.

GREEN TOMATO MINCEMEAT

5½ c. chopped green tomatoes
5½ c. chopped apples
8 c. brown sugar
½ t. cloves
1 t. nutmeg
1 t. cinnamon
2 lbs. chopped raisins
2 t. salt
1 c. chopped suet or ground beef
1 c. vinegar
1 orange rind, grated

Chop tomatoes and drain thoroughly. Measure juice and add an equal amount of water to the pulp. Heat until scalding hot. Drain off liquid. Repeat two times: adding fresh water, scalding and draining. Add the chopped apples to the tomatoes. Add sugar mixed with spices, raisins, salt, and suet. Cook until clear. Add remaining ingredients and cook until mixture thickens and flavors are blended. Pack into hot, sterilized jars and seal.

MINCE PIE WITH OATMEAL CRUST

CRUST

¾ c. flour
½ t. salt
½ c. quick-cooking rolled oats
⅓ c. shortening
4 T. cold water

Sift together flour and salt. Stir in rolled oats. Cut in shortening and sprinkle on cold water. Stir until just dampened. Roll out on floured board and fit into 9-inch pie pan.

FILLING

2½ c. prepared mincemeat
⅓ c. brown sugar
2 T. flour
¾ c. whipping cream
½ c. chopped pecans

Pour mincemeat into unbaked pie shell. Combine brown sugar and flour. Add whipping cream and blend well. Pour cream mixture over mincemeat. Sprinkle with pecans. Bake at 425° for 15 minutes. Reduce heat to 325° and bake 15 to 20 minutes longer or until done.

PUMPKIN-MINCEMEAT PIE

1 unbaked 9-inch pie shell
2 c. cooked pumpkin
¾ c. brown sugar
¾ t. cinnamon
¼ t. nutmeg
⅛ t. ginger
⅛ t. cloves
½ t. salt
2 eggs, beaten
1 c. evaporated milk
1 c. mincemeat

Combine pumpkin, sugar, spices and salt. Add beaten eggs and mix well. Gradually add evaporated milk, stirring until well blended. Set aside. Spread mincemeat over bottom of pie shell. Pour pumpkin mixture over mincemeat. Bake at 375° for 45 minutes or until a metal knife inserted into center of pie comes out clean. Cool. Garnish with whipped cream if desired.

JELLY PUDDING PIE

For each serving desired, use 2 slices homemade bread which has been buttered, sprinkled with sugar and toasted in a slow oven until crisp. Place the toasted bread in a bowl.

When a jelly jar is nearly empty, use a bit of hot water to rinse out the jelly that clings to the jar. Save and pour hot over the toasted bread. Or use a fresh new jar of jelly or preserves—or any leftover fruits. This makes a delicious fruit pudding when doused with rich milk.

CUSTARD PIE

1 unbaked pie shell
3 eggs
½ c. sugar
2 c. milk
1 t. vanilla
⅛ t. salt
Dash of nutmeg

Beat eggs until light and frothy. Add sugar, milk, vanilla and salt. Mix well. Brush pie shell with melted butter. Add custard and sprinkle with ground nutmeg. Bake at 450° for 10 minutes, then reduce heat to 350° and bake for about 40 minutes, or until custard is set.

CHOCOLATE PIE

3 eggs, separated
1 c. sugar
2 T. butter
4 T. cocoa
4 T. flour
2 c. milk
¼ t. salt
2 t. vanilla
3 T. sugar
1 baked 9-inch pie shell

Beat egg yolks until light. Beat in sugar, butter, cocoa and flour. Add milk and salt and cook in double boiler until thick. Add 1 teaspoon vanilla. Pour into baked pie shell. Beat egg whites until stiff. Add 3 tablespoons sugar and 1 teaspoon vanilla. Beat into peaks. Spread on top of pie and bake until brown at 375°.

GRAPE PIE

Pastry for 2-crust 9-inch pie
6 c. Concord grapes
1 c. sugar
¼ c. flour
¼ t. salt
1 t. lemon juice
1 T. butter

Wash and peel grapes, saving skins. Cook pulp in a saucepan with no water; bring to a hard boil. Rub through a strainer to remove seeds. Mix strained pulp with the reserved skins. Mix flour, sugar and salt; stir into grapes. Add lemon juice and butter. Pour into pastry-lined 9-inch pie pan. Top with second crust. Slit top crust and seal edges. Bake at 400° for about 40 minutes or until crust is browned and pie is bubbly.

APPLE-BUTTERSCOTCH PIE

Pastry for 2-crust pie
⅔ c. brown sugar
⅓ c. cream
2 T. flour
¼ t. salt
¼ c. sugar
6 to 8 cooking apples
Juice of ½ lemon

Combine brown sugar and cream and cook in double boiler for 20 minutes. Roll out pie crust and fit into 9-inch pie pan. Mix flour, salt and sugar and sprinkle over the bottom crust. Peel and core apples, slice thin, and fill pie. Squeeze lemon juice into brown sugar-cream mixture. Pour ⅔ of mixture over apples. Cut 2-inch hole in top crust and place over apples; seal edges. Bake 20 minutes at 425°, then reduce heat to 350° and bake 25 minutes more. When baked, pour remaining brown sugar mixture into hole in top crust. Serve warm.

PINEAPPLE CREAM PIE

1 baked 9-inch pie shell
½ c. sugar
3 T. cornstarch
½ t. salt
2½ c. milk
3 eggs, separated
1 T. butter
1 t. vanilla
1 c. crushed pineapple (1 small can)
3 T. sugar
½ t. vanilla

Mix ½ cup sugar, cornstarch and salt. Combine with milk in a heavy saucepan. Beat in egg yolks. Cook over medium heat, stirring constantly, until mixture thickens. Add butter and vanilla; stir in pineapple. Pour mixture into baked pie shell. Beat egg whites until frothy. Add 3 tablespoons sugar and beat until mixture forms soft peaks. Add vanilla. Spread on top of pie filling, being sure to seal edges. Bake at 375° until delicately browned.

BLACKBERRY DEEP DISH PIE

Pastry for single-crust pie
1 qt. fresh blackberries
¾ c. sugar
2½ T. quick-cooking tapioca
¼ t. salt
1 T. butter

Combine blackberries, sugar, tapioca and salt. Pour into an 8-inch square baking dish. Dot with butter. Let stand 15 minutes. Roll pastry ⅛ inch thick (to fit top of baking dish). Cut several slits in center. Place on top of filling. Bake at 425° for 25 minutes. Serve warm.

If you like a beautiful brown crust on your pies, brush the top crust lightly with milk before baking.

Cookies

GOOD COOKIES

1 c. shortening
1 c. brown sugar
1 c. white sugar
2 eggs, beaten
1½ c. flour
1 t. baking powder
1 t. baking soda
½ t. salt
1 T. vanilla
2 c. crisp rice cereal
2 c. quick-cooking rolled oats

Cream shortening and sugars. Add eggs, beating well. Sift flour, baking powder, soda and salt together. Add to egg mixture. Mix in vanilla, rice cereal and rolled oats. Bake at 375° for about 12 minutes.

Cookies

FRUIT PATS

1½ c. sugar
¾ c. shortening
3 eggs, beaten
2 T. sour milk or buttermilk
3 c. flour
1 t. baking soda
½ t. salt
1 t. cinnamon
1 t. vanilla
1 c. whole wheat flour *or* rolled oats
2 c. raisins, washed and drained
1 c. nutmeats

Cream sugar and shortening. Add eggs and beat well. Add sour milk. Sift flour, soda, salt and cinnamon together and stir into first mixture. Add vanilla. Stir in whole wheat flour or rolled oats. Add raisins and nuts. Drop by teaspoonfuls on greased cookie sheet and bake at 375° until brown.

PINEAPPLE CRUNCHIES

1 c. sugar
½ c. shortening
2 eggs, beaten
1½ c. flour
¼ t. baking soda
¼ t. salt
1 t. baking powder
⅜ c. sour cream
1 c. quick-cooking rolled oats
1 c. nuts
1 c. raisins
⅔ c. drained crushed pineapple

Cream sugar and shortening. Add eggs. Sift flour, soda, salt and baking powder together. Add to egg mixture alternately with sour cream. Add remaining ingredients and mix well. Drop by small spoonfuls on greased cookie sheet. Bake at 375° for 10 to 12 minutes.

APPLESAUCE SQUARES

½ c. shortening
1 c. sugar
1 egg, beaten
1 c. raisins, moistened in hot water
   and drained
1 c. applesauce
1 t. baking soda
1½ c. flour
1 t. baking powder
1 t. cinnamon
½ t. salt
½ c. nuts

Cream shortening and sugar. Add beaten egg and mix well. Heat applesauce and add soda while hot. Cool to warm and add to sugar mixture. Sift dry ingredients over nuts and raisins; add to above mixture. Bake in greased cookie sheet at 375° for 20 to 30 minutes or until done. While hot, sprinkle with powdered sugar and cut into squares.

RAISIN HONEY DROPS

¾ c. sugar
¾ c. butter or margarine
¾ c. honey
1 egg
2 c. flour
1 t. cinnamon
1 t. salt
½ t. baking soda
2 c. quick-cooking rolled oats
1 c. raisins

Cream sugar and shortening. Add honey and egg. Sift flour, cinnamon, salt, and soda into creamed mixture. Add rolled oats and raisins. Drop by teaspoonfuls onto baking sheet and bake at 375° for 12 to 14 minutes.

BROWN SUGAR
REFRIGERATOR COOKIES

1 c. butter
1½ c. brown sugar
2 eggs
1 t. vanilla
2 c. flour
2 t. baking soda
2 t. cream of tartar

Cream butter and sugar. Add eggs and vanilla and beat well. Sift together dry ingredients; stir into sugar-butter mixture. Chill. Make into walnut-sized balls and bake at 400° until lightly browned.

OATMEAL CRISPIES

1 c. shortening
1 c. brown sugar
1 c. white sugar
2 eggs, well beaten
1 t. vanilla
1½ c. flour
1 t. salt
1 t. baking soda
3 c. quick-cooking rolled oats
½ c. chopped nuts

Cream shortening and sugars. Beat in eggs and vanilla. Add sifted dry ingredients. Mix in oatmeal and nuts. Shape into rolls. Chill overnight. Slice and bake at 375° for 8 to 10 minutes or until lightly browned.

COCONUT COOKIES

½ c. white sugar
½ c. brown sugar
½ c. shortening
1 egg, beaten
1 c. flour
½ t. salt
½ t. baking powder
½ t. baking soda
1 c. quick-cooking rolled oats
½ c. shredded coconut
½ c. chopped nuts
1 t. vanilla

Cream sugars and shortening. Beat in egg. Sift flour, salt, baking powder and soda together; add to sugar mixture. Blend in rolled oats, coconut, nuts and vanilla. Place on greased cookie sheets, flatten a little and bake at 325° for 15 minutes.

OATMEAL COOKIES

2 c. brown sugar
1 c. shortening
2 eggs
2 c. flour
2 t. baking soda
1 t. baking powder
½ t. salt
3 c. quick-cooking rolled oats
1 t. vanilla
1 c. nuts

Cream the sugar and shortening. Add eggs and beat until creamy. Sift together flour, salt, baking powder and soda. Add to first mixture and blend well. Blend in rolled oats. Add vanilla and nuts. Drop by teaspoonfuls on baking sheet and bake at 375° for about 12 minutes.

NO-BAKE CHOCOLATE OATMEAL COOKIES

½ c. butter or margarine
2 c. sugar
6 T. cocoa
½ c. milk
3 c. quick-cooking rolled oats
1 t. vanilla
½ c. nuts

Place butter in saucepan. Mix sugar and cocoa together and add to butter. Add milk. Heat until butter melts, then boil 4 or 5 minutes. Stir in rolled oats, vanilla and nuts. Drop by teaspoonfuls on waxed paper.

MOLASSES SUGAR COOKIES

¾ c. shortening
1 c. sugar
¼ c. molasses
1 egg, beaten
2 c. flour
2 t. baking soda
1 t. cinnamon
½ t. cloves
¼ t. ginger
½ t. salt

Melt shortening over low heat. Cool. Add sugar, molasses and egg. Beat well. Sift dry ingredients together and add to first mixture. Mix well and chill thoroughly. Form into 1-inch balls, roll in sugar, and place on cookie sheet 2 inches apart. Bake at 375° for 8 to 10 minutes. Makes about 4 dozen cookies.

HARVEST BARS

¼ c. butter
1 c. brown sugar
1 t. vanilla
2 eggs
⅔ c. pumpkin
½ c. chopped dates
½ c. nuts
2 T. flour
½ c. flour
½ t. baking powder
¼ t. baking soda
½ t. salt
½ t. each cinnamon, nutmeg, and ginger

Cream butter, brown sugar, and vanilla together. Add eggs. Beat well and add pumpkin. Dredge dates and nuts in the 2 tablespoons flour. Sift together remaining dry ingredients and add to pumpkin mixture. Add dates and nuts. Bake in greased pan for 30 minutes at 350°. Frost with lemon icing and cut into bars.

LEMON ICING

1½ c. powdered sugar
1 t. lemon flavoring
Cream

Combine sugar and lemon flavoring. Stir in enough cream to spread easily.

CARROT COOKIES

1 c. soft shortening
¾ c. sugar
1 egg
1 c. cooked carrots, mashed
¼ c. milk
1 t. vanilla
½ t. lemon flavoring
2 c. flour
2 t. baking powder
½ t. salt
1 c. bran flakes

Cream shortening and sugar. Add egg and beat well. Stir in carrots, milk and flavorings. Sift flour, baking powder, and salt together and combine with the bran flakes. Add to first mixture and mix well. Drop by teaspoonfuls onto baking sheets and bake at 375° about 18 minutes. Grated raw carrots may be used instead of cooked carrots. Decrease baking time to about 12 minutes. Cookies may be frosted if desired.

FROSTING

1 c. sifted powdered sugar
2 T. orange juice

Beat until smooth and spread on cooled cookies.

For most cookie recipes, it is not necessary to grease the baking sheet. The shortening in the cookies is sufficient.

Pictured opposite
Harvest Bars

COCONUT BARS

½ c. flour
¾ c. brown sugar
½ c. white sugar
½ t. salt
½ t. baking soda
2 eggs, beaten
½ c. grated coconut
½ c. nuts
½ c. powdered sugar, sifted

Sift flour; add sugars, salt and soda. Beat in eggs, nuts and grated coconut. Place in shallow greased pan and bake in 350° oven for 30 minutes. Cut into strips. When cool, roll in powdered sugar.

POPCORN-PEANUT SQUARES

4 qts. popped corn
1 c. peanuts
1½ c. sugar
½ c. corn syrup
½ c. water
1 T. vinegar
1 t. butter
¼ t. baking soda

Force enough freshly popped popcorn through a food chopper, using the medium blade, to make 2 quarts. Grind the peanuts also. Combine sugar, corn syrup, water and vinegar; boil until a little of the mixture cracks when tested in cold water. Remove from heat, add butter and soda, and stir. Pour over the corn and peanuts, mixing thoroughly. Press firmly into a buttered pan so that the mixture is about 1 inch thick. Cut into squares or break into pieces as desired.

SHORTCUT SUGAR COOKIES

¾ c. sugar
2/3 c. shortening
1 egg
2 c. flour
1½ t. baking powder
¼ t. salt
4 t. milk
½ t. vanilla

Cream sugar and shortening together. Beat in egg. Sift together flour, baking powder and salt; add to first mixture. Stir in milk and vanilla. Chill 3 hours. Roll out ¼ inch thick on lightly floured board. Cut into squares or diamonds. Bake on cookie sheets at 375° for 5 to 6 minutes. Cool slightly on cookie sheet before removing to cooling rack.

SOUR CREAM DROP COOKIES

1 c. brown sugar
1 c. white sugar
1 c. shortening
1 c. sour cream
2 eggs, beaten
4½ c. flour
½ t. salt
½ t. nutmeg
½ t. baking soda
3 t. baking powder

Cream sugars and shortening. Add sour cream and beat well. Add eggs and beat in. Sift dry ingredients together and stir into first mixture. Coconut, nuts, or chocolate chips may be added if desired. Drop by teaspoonfuls on greased cookie sheet and bake at 375° for about 12 minutes.

POUND CAKE

1 c. butter or margarine
2 c. sugar
6 eggs
2 c. flour
1 t. vanilla
1 t. almond flavoring
1 t. lemon flavoring

Cream butter and sugar. Add eggs one at a time, beating after each addition. Add sifted flour and flavorings. Bake in angel food pan at 350° nearly an hour.

CHOPPED APPLE CAKE

2 c. sugar
½ c. shortening
2 eggs
4 c. chopped apples
1 c. chopped nuts
2 c. flour
2 t. baking soda
2 t. cinnamon
1 t. nutmeg
1 t. salt

Cream sugar and shortening together. Add beaten eggs and mix well. Add apples and nuts to first mixture but do not stir in. Sift combined dry ingredients over the apples and nuts. Stir all in until thoroughly mixed. This is a very stiff batter. Bake in greased 9" x 13" pan at 350° for 15 minutes. Reduce heat to 325° and bake 25 minutes longer. To serve, cut in squares and top with sauce. Cake may also be served without sauce.

SAUCE

1 c. sugar
½ c. butter or margarine
½ c. light cream or half-and-half

Cook together until thick. Add 1 teaspoon vanilla. Spoon over cake pieces and top with whipped cream.

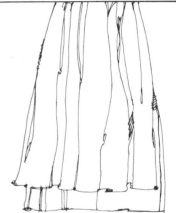

GOLD CAKE

½ c. shortening
1 c. sugar
½ c. milk
8 egg yolks
2 t. lemon extract
⅛ t. salt
2 c. flour
3 t. baking powder

Cream shortening and sugar. Add remaining ingredients and beat vigorously for 3 minutes. Pour into two 8-inch cake pans. Bake at 350° until cake tests done. Note: This is a good way to use up egg yolks left from making angel food cakes, meringues or white cakes.

SPICE CAKE

2 c. flour
½ t. cinnamon
½ t. cloves
¼ t. ginger
2 t. baking powder
¼ t. salt
½ c. shortening
1 c. sugar
2 eggs
¾ c. milk

Sift dry ingredients together. Cream sugar and shortening and beat in eggs until light and fluffy. Add the milk alternately with the flour mixture. Bake in 2 greased 9″ layer pans at 375° for 25 to 30 minutes. May be baked in loaf pan.

GINGERBREAD

½ c. sugar
½ c. shortening
1 c. molasses
1 t. baking soda
1 c. boiling water
2½ c. flour
½ t. cinnamon
½ t. ginger
½ t. cloves
2 eggs, well beaten

Cream sugar and shortening. Add molasses. Dissolve soda in hot water and add to the sugar mixture. Sift flour and spices together and beat in well. Add beaten eggs and mix well. Bake in a 9-inch square pan at 350° for about 40 minutes. Cut in squares and serve hot topped with whipped cream.

APPLE CREAM TOPPING
(for Spice Cake or Gingerbread)

1 c. canned applesauce
½ c. sugar
½ t. cinnamon
1 c. whipping cream

Beat cream until thickened. Add sugar and cinnamon blended together and beat cream until it peaks. Fold in drained applesauce. Chill. Top cut pieces of spice cake or gingerbread.

CREAM CAKE

2 eggs
1 c. sugar
1¼ c. cream
2 c. flour
2 t. baking powder
¼ t. salt
1 t. vanilla

Beat eggs. Add sugar and beat in. Sift flour, baking powder, and salt together and add to egg mixture alternately with the cream. Beat well. Add vanilla. Pour into 2 greased and floured 9″ pans and bake at 350° until cakes test done.

Pictured opposite
Gingerbread

DATE CAKE

1 c. boiling water
1 c. chopped dates
1 t. baking soda
1 c. sugar
⅓ c. softened butter
1 egg
1 t. vanilla
1½ c. flour
1 t. baking powder
½ t. salt
½ c. chopped nuts

Pour boiling water over dates. Stir in soda and allow to cool. Cream sugar and butter. Add egg and vanilla and beat well. Sift flour with baking powder and salt; mix with creamed mixture until well blended. Stir in date mixture. Add nuts. Bake in greased and floured 9" x 13" pan at 350° for 35 minutes.

WHITE CAKE

1½ c. sugar
½ c. butter
2½ c. flour
2 t. baking powder
¼ t. salt
1 c. milk
1 t. vanilla
4 egg whites

Cream sugar and butter. Sift flour, baking powder, and salt together and add alternately with the milk. Add vanilla. Beat egg whites until stiff but not dry and fold in last. Pour into greased 9" x 13" x 2" cake pan. Bake at 375° for about 40 minutes.

TWO EGG CAKE

1 c. sugar
½ c. shortening
1 t. vanilla
2 eggs
2 c. flour
2½ t. baking powder
⅔ c. milk

Cream sugar and shortening. Beat in eggs and add vanilla. Sift flour and baking powder together and add to egg mixture alternately with milk. Beat until smooth. Bake in 2 greased 8" layer pans or make cupcakes. Bake at 350°.

MASHED POTATO CAKE

1 c. shortening
2 c. sugar
4 eggs
1 c. hot mashed potatoes
2 c. flour
3 t. baking powder
½ t. salt
½ c. cocoa
½ t. cinnamon
½ t. cloves
½ c. milk
½ c. nuts

Cream shortening and sugar together. Add eggs one at a time, beating after each addition. Add potatoes and beat until just blended. Sift all dry ingredients together and add alternately with the milk. Fold in nuts. Bake in greased and floured 10" x 13" pan at 350° for 45 minutes.

APPLE CAKE

1⅔ c. sugar
¾ c. butter or margarine
2 eggs
2 large apples, diced
1⅔ c. flour
1 t. baking soda
½ t. salt
1 t. cinnamon
1 t. cloves
½ c. nuts

Cream sugar and butter. Beat in eggs. Add apples. Sift dry ingredients together and add to apple mixture. Beat well. Stir in nuts. Bake in greased 9″ x 13″ pan at 350° for about 30 minutes.

CARAMEL ANGEL CAKE

1½ c. brown sugar
½ c. water
1¼ c. egg whites
¼ t. salt
1 t. cream of tartar
1 t. vanilla
1 c. sifted cake flour

Cook sugar and water until it becomes thick and will spin a thread when dropped from the tip of a spoon (220° F.). Beat egg whites with salt until frothy. Add cream of tartar and beat until whites are stiff but not dry. Pour sugar syrup slowly over egg whites, beating continuously until all the syrup is used. Fold flour in gradually. Add vanilla and pour into ungreased angel food pan. Bake at 300° for an hour, or until cake tests done.

RED DEVIL'S FOOD CAKE

1 c. sugar
1¾ c. cake flour
⅓ c. cocoa
1¼ t. baking soda
1 t. salt
½ c. soft shortening
1 c. milk
2 eggs
1 t. vanilla

Blend together sugar, flour, cocoa, soda and salt. Add shortening and ⅔ cup of milk and beat 2 minutes. Beat in remaining ingredients. Bake in greased and floured 9″ x 13″ x 2″ pan at 350° for 30 to 45 minutes.

OATMEAL COCOA CAKE

1½ c. boiling water
1 c. quick-cooking rolled oats
½ c. shortening
1½ c. sugar
2 eggs
1 t. vanilla
1 c. flour
½ t. salt
1 t. baking soda
½ c. cocoa

Pour boiling water over rolled oats. Set aside. Cream sugar and shortening. Add eggs and vanilla and beat well. Add rolled oats mixture. Sift dry ingredients together and beat in. Bake in greased 9″ x 13″ pan at 350° for 35 minutes.

To turn cake layers out of the pans easily, grease the pans well, then dust with flour before pouring in the batter and baking. An alternative is to grease the bottom of the pan, cover with waxed paper, and grease again. In either case, cut around the edge with a knife and invert onto cake rack while hot.

BUTTERMILK CAKE

2 c. sugar
½ c. shortening
½ c. butter or margarine
5 eggs, separated
1 c. buttermilk
1 t. vanilla
2 c. flour
1 t. baking soda
1 t. salt
2 c. coconut
1 c. chopped nuts

Cream sugar, shortening and butter or margarine. Add the egg yolks and beat well. Add buttermilk and vanilla. Sift flour, soda, and salt together and add to first mixture. Beat well. Add coconut and nuts. Beat the egg whites stiff and fold into the batter. Pour into 3 greased and floured layer cake pans. Bake at 350° for 35 to 40 minutes.

FROSTING

2 c. sifted powdered sugar
¼ c. butter or margarine (softened)
1 t. vanilla
Buttermilk

Mix all ingredients together, using just enough buttermilk to make spreading consistency. Beat smooth. Spread between layers and top and sides of cake.

QUICK CHOCOLATE CAKE

1½ c. sugar
4 T. cocoa
½ c. butter
1 c. milk
2 eggs, beaten
1½ c. flour
1 t. baking soda
½ c. cold coffee

Mix sugar and cocoa in a saucepan. Cream butter into this mixture. Add milk and cook until smooth. Let cool. When cool add eggs, flour, soda and coffee. Beat well. Bake in greased shallow 9" x 13" pan at 350° until done when tested with a toothpick. Remove from oven and cover with icing while warm.

CHOCOLATE ICING

2 c. sifted powdered sugar
6 t. cocoa
4 T. soft butter
Dash of salt
3 T. cold coffee
½ t. vanilla

Mix together powdered sugar and cocoa. Add remaining ingredients and beat smooth. Spread on cake.

CARROT CAKE

1 c. margarine
2 c. sugar
1½ c. grated raw carrots
1 c. nuts
1 T. grated orange rind
3 c. flour
3 t. baking powder
1 t. cinnamon
1 t. nutmeg
½ t. salt
⅔ c. orange juice
4 egg whites, stiffly beaten

Cream margarine and sugar. Add carrots, nuts and orange rind. Sift dry ingredients together and blend into carrot mixture alternately with the orange juice. Fold in egg whites last. Bake in greased and floured 10-inch tube pan at 350° for 60 to 70 minutes. Cool in pan 20 minutes, then turn out of pan onto rack to completely cool.

PUMPKIN CAKE

4 eggs
2 c. sugar
1 c. salad oil
2 c. flour
½ t. salt
2 t. cinnamon
2 t. baking soda
2 c. cooked or canned pumpkin

Beat eggs. Add sugar and oil. Sift dry ingredients and add to egg mixture. Blend in pumpkin. Pour into greased and floured tube pan. Bake at 350° for 1 hour. Remove from oven. Let stand 10 minutes before removing from pan to cool.

COLD WATER CHOCOLATE CAKE

½ c. butter or margarine
1 c. sugar
1 t. vanilla
⅛ t. salt
½ c. cocoa
⅓ c. cold water
2½ c. flour
1¼ t. baking soda
1 c. cold water
3 egg whites
¾ c. sugar

Cream together the butter and sugar. Add vanilla and salt. Combine the cocoa with the ⅓ cup of cold water. Mix well and add to the creamed mixture. Sift flour and soda together and add to the creamed mixture alternately with the 1 cup cold water. Beat until just blended after each addition. If using an electric mixer, set at medium speed. Beat the egg whites until stiff but not dry. Add the ¾ cup sugar gradually, beating after each addition. Fold egg whites into batter. Bake in 10" x 14" greased pan at 350° until cake tests done.

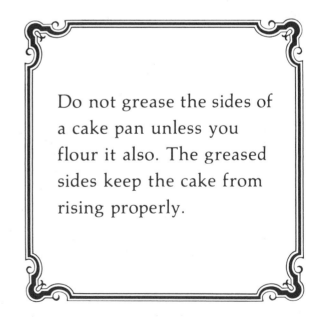

Do not grease the sides of a cake pan unless you flour it also. The greased sides keep the cake from rising properly.

INDEX

Continued on page 63

MAMA'S KITCHEN

The smell of cookies baking
Brings back thoughts of Mama's kitchen;
Her suppers were so tasty
We could hardly keep from snitchin'.
Fresh-baked bread and apple pie,
Beef or chicken dishes;
Noodle soup to chocolate cake—
Her meals were just delicious.
But, oh, what fun it was to watch
As Mama stirred and measured.
Helping her to cook and bake
Were moments that I treasured.
Meals that were prepared with love—
These memories I'm rich in.
It's certain that no feasts compare
To those from Mama's kitchen!

SX517 BOOK VIEWER STAND—The modern see-through book stand, made of strong, durable Lucite, completely protects cookbooks and other display items from smudges and dirt. The stand conveniently folds flat for easy storage or hanging. It's perfect for use in the kitchen, workshop, or home study. A great gift idea and it's only $3.00, plus 50¢ postage.

editor
Maryjane Hooper Tonn

•

managing editor
Ralph Luedtke

•

associate editor
Julie Hogan

•

photographic editor
Gerald Koser

•

production editor
Stuart L. Zyduck

Other Cookbooks Available

Designed by

Ellen Hohenfeldt